# I'M STILL HERE...

## I'M NOT DONE YET

JEAN THOMPSON

HOV
PUBLISHING

# I'M STILL HERE... I'M NOT DONE YET

HOV Publishing a division of HOV, LLC.
www.hovpub.com
hopeofvision@gmail.com

Contact the author Jean Thompson
Email: jeaniemari@gmail.com

Cover Design: Hope of Vision Designs
Cover Photos Credits:

Editors: HOV Publishing

For more information about special discounts for bulk purchases, please contact Jean Thompson or HOV Publishing

ISBN: 978-1-955107-71-6

10  9  8  7  6  5  4  3  2  1

Printed in the United States of America

# DEDICATION

This book was written in loving memory of three precious women I adored: my mother Jeanette Evelyn Thompson, and two older sisters Joanne A. Mobley and Sharon E. Thompson. They provided me with unconditional love, support, and strength to keep going.

These ladies have all taken a piece of my heart with them. If only they were still here to see this huge accomplishment.

May they REST IN PEACE until we meet again.

Love always. Mommy, Podie, and Shay.

Thanks to my Grandpa George Cook and Grandma Patricia Cook. May they REST IN PEACE.

# ACKNOWLEDGEMENTS

Glory and honor belong to God, he did it all for me. My relationship with the highest is to serve him and hold on to his promises to never leave, nor forsake me. Phil 4:13, *"I can do all things through Christ which strengtheneth me."* God can and will use you for his glory; he will turn your mess into a message.

Thank you to my children Nakiya, Tiffany, Travis, and my grandson Dior. I'm forever grateful to them for pushing me past my boundaries and consistently being my cheer squad. My children are the roadmap to my success; constantly helping me stay on course. They are responsible for my strength and endurance. I am determined to be all God has created me to be. God has a great journey for each of you and I will be here for you always. You can count on that. Trust, believe in Jesus and reach for greatness.

# SPECIAL SHOUT-OUTS

A special shout-out to my Georgia Crew: Shaquana, Jessica, Chanelle (Jaffah), and D'ontay. My nieces and nephews down south rally for my success and inspire me to excel in all I do. My sister Joanne had faith in me to be there for her children. In my last conversation with her, she said, "take care of my babies." Now I never miss their graduations, school performances, or acting auditions. The holidays in Georgia are amazing. Our entire family sits around, eat, play games, and stay up late at night.

I give blessings to their children as well: De'Shaquan, Jasun, Jada, Quianna, Nevaeh, Mason, and Malikai. Sharon's son, Saquan, you are unique in your own way.

Fond endearments of my 3 living siblings: Frederick, Cheryl, and Lisa. I want to share all my Nieces and Nephews with you and let them know that you can achieve anything you put your mind to. For

Jamel, Shaun, Tyshawn (RIP), Lateeshia, Shanida, Oginga, Lamar, Christopher, Naquan, Quasia, Antwon, Nasiah, Jalen, Shaun Jr, Efren, Oshyn, Shawnae, Kamar, Terry J, Alisha, Shawn III, Maurice, Jayden, Kamaree, Azzareya, Niahla, Lexi, Tiana, Oginga Jr, Odessy, and Daniel.

My one and only Uncle George Cook, his wife Stephanie, sons Corey, George III, and daughter Pearlasha. I love you so much as if we were siblings. We grew up in the same household where food was plentiful and with a mom who was passionate about ironing. She made bedsheets crisp, and sometimes, even ironed our underwear (inside family joke).

# TABLE OF CONTENTS

# THE EARLY YEARS

Being a woman is not easy, but it is very much rewarding. Being a single mother of two daughters and one son, I have seen it all and have been through it all. From an early age, I was always interested in heels, purses, and makeup. Girly things were always at the top of the list of things I wanted. I acquired my first genuine Coach bag at fourteen years old. My mom said I could purchase it with my first summer youth job paycheck. That was a huge deal for me.

# MY SISTER'S FOOTSTEPS

I followed in the footsteps of my two older sisters. I wanted whatever they had. They had jobs and could buy a lot of fancy things, so I wanted the same. Even at a young age, I tried doing all the things they did, like smoking cigarettes and partying. One day when I caught them smoking, I wanted to do the same, not realizing they were bad for our health. Mom was not happy with them when she found out they gave me my first cigarette. I started to enjoy it. I smoked more, and by the time I was sixteen years old, I started drinking beer.

# OBSERVANT

On another day, a few of my girlfriends and I planned a Saturday night out. We went to a club where the music was so loud, we could not hear each other speak. Some guys at the club asked if we wanted to dance and have drinks. I refused. I never let guys buy my drinks at clubs. Thankfully, (and gratefully), I was cautious. When I got my drink, I drank it right where I was. My girlfriend left her drink and came back for it later, but by that time, one of the guys spiked her drink. Later that night, he tried to attack her in the lady's bathroom. From that time and on, I always warn women to never buy drinks and leave them unattended. Even though I was a young woman, I was observant and discerning about danger lurking.

# SHAME FOR REPUTATION

I grew up a lot faster than I may have wanted to. It was not the way I wanted to. At the tender age of eight years old, I was physically and verbally assaulted by a male cousin and an uncle. The abuse went on for years because I was afraid and too embarrassed to share that horrific experience with my family. One day, I decided to inform my oldest sister about what took place throughout those years.

She said I could have told her about it when it happened, and I told her about how I was too scared to do it. I did not want the family to separate or be ridiculed by our neighbors. At that time, our family had a great reputation in the community. If word got out, imagine what the talk about us would have been like in those days? Incest running rampant in my family? That would have been unheard of! The unwanted actions by those two family members taught me later in my life to be very cautious about bringing new guys around my daughters. I never allowed my daughters to spend the night out, except if they were at my mother's or sister's house. I never let men spend the night at my house. I wanted to make sure my son and daughters would always be safe in their own home. The experience of being physically and verbally abused as a young child became a mental strain that affected my life for years after. It took some time for me to begin relationships, and it was that much harder for me to trust men.

# A CLOSED HEART

I was a guarded young woman. My heart was closed off, but the time came when I decided to begin dating and learning to trust. I was sixteen years old when I met a young man who would become the father of my first daughter. He was working in a diner where I went to have lunch after school was out. He was the manager, and he would come over to take my order where I sat at the counter. He was a mature, very good-looking, charming, and charismatic guy. We exchanged phone numbers and he promised to give me a call. Before we made a date to go out, I had my family check him out. I invited my older sister to go with me to his diner, and we sat and talked for a while. She agreed that he was good looking but noticed that he was a little older than me. She was ok with me going out to dinner with him, but she also told me to be sure not to leave my food and drink unattended.

# HE DECEIVED ME

The next weekend, I went out on a date with him to a local park during the daytime so we could walk, talk, and get to know each other. I figured late nights were too inviting and might lead to other ideas. We continued to see each other and dated for about a year. In the beginning, he was kind and caring. He bought me flowers and boxes of candy for many of our dates. He even started to splurge lots of his paychecks on me with pretty heels and purses. He knew exactly how to keep me smiling. Every week when we went out, we were dressed to the nines with our jackets and shoes in matching colors (and a new purse for me). I really fell for this guy, and he said he felt the same about me. I felt his love for me too. I thought I hit the jackpot. My friends were so happy and elated that I was the first among us to be in a great relationship. He met my mom and siblings, as I had already met his mom and extended family. We thought we were ready to start a family, so we decided to consummate our relationship. I had one more year left in high school, and he was working and already had his own place. Everything was falling into place. We had enough room for a newborn, and he was saving money to get ready for parenthood. He was so overprotective of me. He never allowed me to go see friends or be at many of our family functions. I thought that was a good thing at the time…until he became more jealous and aggressive with me. We were always around each other, and the relationship became very strained during the later months of my pregnancy. He became physically aggressive and very volatile at times. I was under the impression he was tired from the long work hours. I also thought it was about me not having food cooked by the time he got in sometimes, but I was sick and tired most times due to the pregnancy. He became absolutely controlling, domineering, and mentally intimidating. My girlfriends were not allowed to come to visit. I kept my mom in the dark about what went on because I wanted her to think I was okay and could be on my own. After my daughter was born and I felt stronger, I knew I had to get away because I felt like a prisoner in my own home. I knew this relationship was over when he burned my leg with a hot iron. I almost killed him that night. I left him bleeding on the floor with a cut to his throat. I had to get out of that house because

I was either going to die or go to jail and what would have happened to my child? My Mom was all I could think about. She moved far away, but he did not know where she moved to. My eldest sister also lived in the same neighborhood as Mom, so they gave me shelter. I left my baby in my mom's care while I went to work. It was not easy, but I was able to get back up again.

# HE SAVED ME

Worship of the Lord was instilled in me at an early age. My great-grand-mother took me and my sisters to church every Sunday. Mom worked hard as a registered nurse. A lot of the weekends were filled with overtime, but she was still able to raise six children and keep a diligent schedule for us. She made sure that we read and studied the word of God. She prayed for us every morning and night, always telling us to keep God first in all situations and circumstances. I thank God for leading and guiding me in all my ways. I almost lost my life being in a dangerous and tumultuous relationship, but God saved me. I had to get free because I had a nervous breakdown during that relationship, but the Lord restored my mental capacity. He gave me the strength and courage to get back up again.

# OUT OF THE BLUE

Some years later, I was able to find a beautiful apartment for me and my daughter to live in. With just the two of us, we lived, laughed, and loved together. My life flourished with beauty and luster for a few years, and then out of the blue, I met an Army soldier through a girlfriend. He was tall, dark, handsome, a terrific cook, and very good with children. He courted me like a gentleman by holding the car door open and pulling out a chair for me at restaurants and such. Then there were the roses that came for birthdays, Mother's Day and other holidays or celebrations. We spoke late nights by telephone and wrote letters to each when we were apart. My daughter loved him. He had so much patience with her and helped out with her math homework. He was a great mathematician and worked out the problems quickly with her. We stayed together for years while we discussed future plans for marriage and more children. We were married in July 1981. We had a small guest list of family and close friends. In August 1983, my second daughter was born. I never had to lift a thing doing any housework. He did it all. He never complained about it or did it grudgingly. We joined and attended church together as a family. He was raised by both his parents, and he exhibited their characteristics. In making our family his priority, he led by example. He was an amazingly sweet dad to his girls, speaking highly of them to others. He loved me and treated with the utmost respect. In 1988, our son was born. He was the child who sealed our marriage. Our relationship was full and complete.

# NOT AGAIN

During these early years, I was smitten by his love of family. I believed he had no wrongdoing, but I guess he began to get bored with the commitment. I became displeased at him for not coming straight home on the weekends. I had no idea about what kept him so captivated outside our home. He went out and partied more and more with his friends. He began to exhibit some aggression towards me about how I was raising our children and made minor complaints about my work hours because he wanted me to be home more. He became unfaithful as a husband. Our house phone rang at all hours of the day, and the person calling hung up as soon as I answered. He became violent with me if I questioned his late-night whereabouts. Once again, the physical abuse began. I felt like I needed to find a safe shelter for me and the children, so after I secured another apartment, I left all the children's clothes and beds behind. I had to start from scratch. I knew if I stayed there, I might not get out alive this time around. I prayed day and night for God to save me and my children. I was in the same cycle I had been in before, but with the Lord on my side, I would not lose. Thank God he stopped attending the church we went to. As for me and the children, we still attend that same church to this day.

# GOD'S PLAN FOR ME

My life transitioned once again, from being a married mother of three to becoming a hardworking single mother. With the struggles, obstacles, depression, and nervous breakdown, things were not easy, but I held on with my three children by my side. I had to show strength and courage to be able to get back up again. When I went through the divorce, I remained strong and resilient for my children. I believed God allowed all this to happen because he knew I was strong. I am a soldier in the army of the Lord, and I can do all things through Christ which strengthens me. The Lord knew the plans he had for my life. It was planned well before I was born. God planned everything to get me to where I am today.

# I AM POWERFUL

As a woman, I am powerful, dynamic, and unique in my own way. I was not a perfect wife, nor a perfect mother, but I would not change my life for anything in the world. With dignity and strength, I raised three great young people. I made some mistakes along the way, but the Lord made my crooked lines straight. For all advisement and correction, I depended on the Lord only, and he never steered me wrong. The Lord turned my hurt and pain into faith, healing, and comfort. He taught me how to forgive myself and others. He taught me how to kick the dust of my shoes and keep moving. The storms in my life were there to make me stronger. My past has refined me for a better future. I thank God for the strength and courage to be able to get back up again. I needed to share this story because I know some young woman is going through the same things I endured. God has more work for me to do.

# ABOUT THE AUTHOR

Jean Thompson is a Brooklyn, New York native. For the last twenty-one years, she has been employed with the New York City Police Department. She holds a baccalaureate degree in child psychology from the College of New Rochelle. Jean is a single mother of three adult children (Nakiya, Tiffany, Travis), and grandmother to Dior Nehemiah Bruce. She is a devoted mother, sister, aunt, and an amazing godmother to nine children. She enjoys spending lots of time with family. With a heart of gold, Jean is a giving person. She is a devoted Christian who has attended her church for over twenty-five years. She is a youth Sunday school teacher, serves on the mothers' board, and leads the church's praise and worship team. In her spare time, Jean enjoys reading, crocheting, and traveling. She has a passion for cooking foods from different cuisines. She is a very active, healthy, and productive woman who has many goals and dreams to pursue in her life. God is not done with her yet.

You can find Jean on:

Facebook: JeanThompson

Instagram: JeanieRoseNYC

LinkedIn: JeanThompson

# SPECIAL THANKS

Thank you to Pastor Elder Mattie Davenport of New York and 2nd St. James Church of Christ. You provide love and guidance in teaching the word of God not only to me, but my children, grandson, and the community. I pray you will reach higher levels in teaching and learning more about how to reach the masses. I truly appreciate all that you do.

Thank you, Dr. Tenaria Drummond -Smith, founder and CEO, of AWOTM, for believing in me.

I have a plethora of stories to tell and she always says, "Don't let those stories go untold." Speak your truth and write it down now. She said the stories you tell, can free someone else.

Thanks so much, Dawn Grantham aka "DGINSPIRES" for your inspiration and encouragement to stay as my bookend (inside joke). You were always there to listen with patience when I wasn't sure what to write about.

Thank you, Cousin Celeste King, for all the late-night talks and your down to earth realness.

I'm grateful and honored to be the God mom of many young adults who depend on me to guide them with a non-judgmental ear and unconditional love. Shamaine, Bernadette, Michelle, Daja, Diamone, Johnathan, Joshua, Luisito, and Evekiel.

Thank you, Germaine Miller-Summers and the HOV Publishing staff for all the dedicated time you put into making this book a bestseller.

To my family and friends, I truly thank you all for the support.

From Amazon Bestselling
Co-Author

# Jean Thompson

 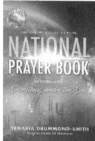 

*Available at*

CPSIA information can be obtained
at www.ICGtesting.com
Printed in the USA
LVHW052236140723
752120LV00016B/1084